Unmistakably Human

Also by Reese Lieberman

this world from my 2 eyez

Unmistakably Human

A collection of poems

Reese Lieberman

Dedicated to each & every remarkable person
who has shown me
how beautiful it is to be human

Preface

       Loss can mean decay, grief, being fully and truly lost yourself. We've all experienced it in one way or another. For me, 2022 meant losing my home to a hurricane. On that night in late September, rain was pouring in through the ceiling and into the walls. I have experienced my fair share of hurricanes thus far in my life, but this one was like nothing I'd ever experienced before. Our whole home was shaking, as was I, while gusts ravaged the shoreline. My family was inside, trying our best to stop the oncoming tides of water and salvage what we could. It was a night caught in the balance of whatever the storm was going to bring, seeing no stars out there in the darkness. The winds screamed much as I did when the house began to be torn apart at the seams. Yet the rain stopped pouring after what felt like an eternity. The skies were gray, but the wind settled down to a brisk breeze. It was hard to even process what had happened. It felt like something out of the worst of my nightmares. But I was wide awake. The power was out for a week afterward. It was still hard to breathe, but the fear dissipated as my body and mind began to recognize that we had all survived, though that took some time to fully settle in, because life looked nothing like it had before. I distinctly remember the first day after the storm in which the sun rose and the skies were purely blue, birds were singing, and it was the sweetest tune I had ever heard.

       As I am writing this, on a humid evening in March of 2023, with Spring just around the corner, I'm still not sure if I have completely processed it.

It's a very strange feeling to know that I will never again step foot in the place that was my home for a decade of my life. The extent of the destruction went beyond the frame of a house, as the place we had so many memories in, and the battle to try and save what was already beyond saving. My hometown will never look the same after part of it fell into the sea. This experience has greatly influenced me, as a person and as a writer. It is a theme you will find throughout this book. But I want you to know, I have become well acquainted with both the dark side and the light side of nature in this past year. And still, I look for the latter.

I may have lost a lot, but I didn't lose the love that I had. I didn't lose the curiosity and awe with which I've always looked at this world. I may have lost the roof over my head, but still my feet are planted in this earth. And yours are too. Through all the darkness, the sun kept rising. And I'm still standing, as is my family, the true lights in my life. Not in spite of, but especially because of my recent experiences with the dark side of nature, I wanted to highlight the light in this book. It took me some time to find it. Writing this book was one of the steps in my search. Everybody has had more than their fair share of losses, and whatever loss means for you, this book is for you. If you feel like through all of this chaos and loss, you have lost a little bit of yourself, know that it's not gone forever. Dear reader, if you take one thing from this book, take this: whatever you might be going through, you can make it through. I believe it because I lived to tell these stories, and you will live to tell your own stories too.

Reese Lieberman

i want to live a life
so filled with love
it pours into the cracks
and crevices
of everything i do

Table of Contents

Introduction

I think it's beautiful that beauty exists even if nobody sees it. You can choose to see it. I think it's beautiful that you can be it. You can wake in the morning with a smile on your face. You can love this world. And sunshine. And books. And people. And you can be one of those people. And you needn't wait a minute to start. I think it's beautiful that to see the beauty in this world is to love it. And love really is a beautiful thing.

This collection of poems is a love letter, an ode to the beauty of being human. It is meant to highlight the most wonderful parts, like our capacity to love, learn, and become better in every moment, with every choice. We are small and the world is large, yet our energy transcends time and space. Our choices echo and reverberate. The possibilities are endless, the probabilities irrelevant. And one way or another, this book wound up in your hands. I hope it touches your heart in some way, like a steaming cup of tea on a brisk winter day or a warm hug from a loved one. And never forget, you are capable of anything you set your mind to because you are human.

"How wonderful it is that nobody need wait a single moment before starting to improve the world."

Anne Frank

Unmistakably Human

Isn't it a beautiful thing
when you feel so much pure joy
you don't know what to do
laughter, tears,
it all comes pouring out of you

It is so unmistakably human,
so untaintedly true
It is raw — not like a wound
but just as the ocean
under the light of the moon
at the coastline on the edge
of the dune
a sunflower in full bloom

the earth whispers

the earth whispers
in sunrises,
stretching her luminous lips
not loud
but crisp

the earth whispers
in seasons,
the effortless, perpetual
order of things
from auburn leaves, to icicles on trees,
to birds finally stretching their wings,
to so much sunshine
you wish
you could bottle it up and save it for
next time
the weather wades into cooler waters

we are mother earth's sons and daughters
and she whispers
oh how she whispers
in rainbows,
in rain storms, in the powerful
(yet we dare to forget its presence)
force of gravity,
in the waves falling and rising in the sea,
following patterns just as those
in our bodies as
we breathe
lungs, heart, throat, mouth, and the breeze

that brushes past the teeth
mother earth whispers,
she did today, she has tonight
and she will tomorrow,
in little fragments of life and light

Just a Little Bit

Maybe we are all just learning and growing,
making mistakes along the way
but we keep going
never really knowing,
just thinking and feeling and doing,
and hopefully improving
just a little bit everyday,
just a little bit means an awful lot,
anyway

an observance of harmony

i never believed in perfection
i thought it was a myth
but that was before i had lived
through a night like this

the stars came out at just the right moment
waves in the sea crashed
and my tears stopped flowing
the moon was glowing

the night was perfect
without even knowing
and then i wondered
what of this world is not perfect
besides that which we do not notice?

well on that night i noticed everything
the salt in the breeze
the moonlight shining on the seas
the shadows that animated the trees
the way all of nature seemed to fall to its knees

there was no fight or fuss
just the breeze flowing through the lush
even the cicadas hushed
in observance of the harmony
which gently rushed
like rain through the gutter
it made my heart flutter
and my mind stutter

then suddenly one thought became clear to me
like lightning piercing through thunder
like being hit by a bus
nature is sacred to nature
why is it not sacred to us?

I like being gentle

I like being gentle
I like that my skin is soft
I like that my lips are a light shade of pink
when I take the glossy lipstick off
I like that my hair curls up tightly in spirals
and I like my facial mist in the mornings —
witch hazel and rose petals
I like drinking chamomile tea in the evening after
heating it up in my sister's blue kettle
I like being human
and I like being gentle
and I love that I can't think of anything better

15

Water pours in,
a leak in the roof became
a leak in the walls
walls, that once held
everything together
are ripping apart at the seams
seams in my pajamas
conceal the shaking of the
body beneath
beneath this veil of darkness
& terror I see no light
light in the distance is
getting closer, the bolts
accompanied by thunder
thunder shakes the ground
& fills my ears
ears still ringing from the
sound of the fire alarm
blaring because water has
found its way into every
inch & wire of this home
home doesn't rhyme with doom
but it does rhyme with bone
bone deteriorates
deteriorates any sense
of hope & happy endings
endings keep coming
coming, the wind whips ferociously
ferociously this storm isn't done
done is the damage
but there's more to come

& we're trapped inside this
broken mess
broken messes crumble
beneath my feet
feet unprepared for any of this,
but ready to run
run my hands through my hair
nervously
nervously nearly forget
how to breathe
breathing gets harder but I
let out a scream
scream like the wind
as it all falls apart
a part of this damage has been
acquired over time
time is moving like aged
turpentine
turpentine tears drip down
my face
faces around me tell me
they feel it too
too much, too fast, no one
could prepare for this
this is the end of more than I know
no one can stop this storm
storms pass eventually
but not without damage
damaging how quickly the world
topples down around me
me, frightened & fifteen
fifteen hours ago
I was so much younger
than I am now

They Say Time Heals But

Nobody teaches you
that there are some mornings
in which the sun
won't rise,
the skies refuse to turn blue
& nature is brutal
all the way through
An unparalleled force
diminishes what once was
beautiful,
what would you do if everything
you had was no more?
Swept up in a storm
you were lucky to survive —
there are some things you
can't prepare for,
some wounds don't heal with time

Duality

I've tasted lightning on my tongue
& it burned with its fierce & fiery heat
I've also tasted sunshine
& it revived me with its warmth,
soft & sweet
What a destructive & divine duality
in this scary, wonderful life we lead
ever-unpredictable is this friendly, fickle
reality
every day invites millions of possibilities
8 billion stories are being written
as we speak,
& as for mine
the warm embraces, the deep & magical
laughter, the sunshine —
those parts will be written in bold
The lightning strikes, the ravenous wind,
the gushing rain,
imprinted with tea stains & through blurry
eyes
those parts will be well-read in time
but it is the love that got me through
the dark & scary nights
that will be <u>underlined</u>

Just Like Oxygen

What do you think of
when you hear birdsong
in the morning?
What about when you see
butterflies swarming?
I think how wonderful
it is to exist
in a beautiful world
where there are days
like this
The calm *after* the storm,
when the weather is warm
with cool undertones
It is finally Fall and I
can feel it in my bones
The skies are blue,
without a cloud in sight
and it's breezy
On days like this,
seeing the beauty
in this world is easy
and on the days when it
is not
I haven't forgot
that though it is more
difficult to see
it is always there
just like oxygen in this
Autumn air

Wide Eyes and Wonder

Have you ever stopped and thought
about just how precious this life we live is?

How quickly flowers bloom and wilt?

It is on this principle that the universe
was built

things are born, they live, and they die

While this life is being lived we are
meant to thrive

While our hearts beat, our lungs breathe,
our eyes blink, we are alive

we are supposed to experience
the vast beauty of this world
with wonder

the sunshine, the starry skies,
and the thunder

We are meant to love,
to love this life and each other
and the skies that we live under

We are made to chase our dreams
like our shadows chase us

We are meant to live so loudly
that though the tide can wash away
our footprints
it cannot erase us

We were born to love the skies
that we live under
with wide eyes and wonder

When You Treat This World With Love

You say you don't like feeling small,
but there's no way to avoid it
because it is the inevitable
but you know what the best thing to
do is?
To love,
to love truly
love people and the world and yourself
you will notice a difference
in the way you speak
when you speak with love
in the way you feel,
your hands whether interlaced with
another's,
baking, or painting various colors
can be simultaneously strong
and soft
you darling, beautiful paradox
Small acts are bigger than you think,
so make sure yours are acts of kindness
When you treat this world with love
you will start to see raindrops the way
others see diamonds,
smiles as precious as gold
and the sound of laughter will never
grow old

A Reminder

Take a breath
You are doing your best
It is okay to rest
Let the weight off your chest
It is okay
if all you do today
is stay
at home
Sometimes you get burnt
by the sun's beautiful,
brutal rays
It is okay
if you step outside tonight
and gaze at the moon
at its gentle, luminescent
sight
It is okay
if you need a little light
and it is okay
if it takes a little time
for you to find it,
happiness isn't a race
just as long as a smile
eventually finds its way
to your face
Darling, we are on a rock
in outer space

How To Find The Beauty Within

Start by loving your cup of coffee
in the morning
or tea in the mid-afternoon,
stepping outside more,
enjoying the view,
at night gazing up at the silver moon
Next, be sure to laugh
at least twice a day
and be mindful of the things you say,
remember kindness goes a long,
long way
After that, listen to the songbirds,
feel the sunlight on your skin
and the rain when it comes pouring in
Smell a flower,
perhaps press its delicate petals
in the pages of a book
Sing in the shower,
go for a drive with the windows down,
laugh out loud,
make others laugh with you
Write a letter,
find little ways every day to be better
Don't take yourself so seriously,
it's okay
if you are not perfectly comfortable
in your skin
Sing a song, take a walk,
read the books on your shelf —

love your life
and along the way
you will learn to love yourself

How to be free

look at the wildflowers grow
watch the clouds unfold
and waves crash in the undertow

listen to the sounds of the world turning
watch as the skies fade and change
smell the spring air,

appreciate this moment,
for it will not last forever
like waves forming in the ocean, there are always
more on their way
but no two moments will ever be the same

watch the sunsets
dance in the rain
some chances come once in a lifetime
some chances come, and may never come again

so smile, and laugh, and cry,
and breathe the same air that the wildflowers breathe
be, just be
and perhaps then you'll be free

Do Not Let the Books Collect Dust

Bend the pages,
stain them yellow
Write notes for later,
underline words and places
you do not know
Highlight the phrases
you like best,
and the ones hardest
to digest

Fall asleep with a book
in your hands
or leave it open
on your nightstand
until you pick it up again
at dawn or at dusk

but whatever you do, do not
let the books on your shelves
collect dust

To Be Understood

We highlight our favorite quotes in the books we read
we make playlists of our favorite songs
we write poetry and stories
we hang posters on our walls
we make books full of our memories
and stack them on our shelves
perhaps it is how we try to understand this world
or perhaps it is in hopes that this world will
understand ourselves

Sweet 16

The sunrise on the day that
marks my sixteenth year on this planet
was sweet,
the whole sky painted vibrant hues
of orange & pink,
the soap smelled of chamomile &
lavender in the sink,
the smiles on my sisters' face,
my father's embrace,
my mother's energy & warm eyes,
my grandmother's handwriting & words,
my sisters' birthday cards a reminder
that they know me so well
& will always be on my side,
my grandfather's jokes & loving heart
Turns out sixteen really was
sweet this year,
even after our home was torn apart,
this family pulled itself together
though we may not have a home
in the sense of shelter
we have rebuilt it in the sense of
memories & love
Sixteen doesn't feel bitter like black tea
it's the cream,
it's the hugs, it's the colors,
it is sweet

Roots

the days pass by quietly
sneaking out the back door without a sound
follow them out
open the window, walk through the screen door
there's a whole world out there to explore
gardens, flowers blossoming, honey bees,
a beautiful breeze
four seasons, eight phases of the moon
I think it'll be a crescent soon
and the air is crisp, the temperature is changing
just watch as the whole world is rearranging
bears going into hibernation
squirrels stocking up on acorns
farmers shifting their crops
I'm swapping flip flops
for boots
trees are holding tightly to their roots
and I think I am too

In Downpours Trees Rise

Peaches ripen
in golden sunlight
but it is in downpours
that trees which
bear these fruits
grow **deep** and **untouchable**
roots

The Beauty of the Storm

Isn't is strange
how quickly things change?
When you think what is now
is to remain,
like the sun is shining,
a rainbow is forming,
and you have finally gotten through
the worst of the rain
it turns out to be the eye of a hurricane
It is calm in the center,
so much so you might think
the storm has passed
but don't be tricked it's not over yet,
so keep your distance from the walls
and stay away from the glass
The storm is not done,
it is still forming in the sea
I could beg and plea,
asking it to have mercy on me
but I already know that nothing
lasts forever,
hurricanes are bound to pass by
eventually
and the beauty of the storm
is that we're all in it together

Haze

The world hasn't been soft lately
the spots I used to look to for sunshine
are shady
The skies are hazy
Street lights are fading
Life is not as luminescent as it once was
The glitter on the creases of my eyelids
is tarnished by the dust
in my lungs

& then the sun came out

Lighting struck the ground,
thunder shook the house,
and when I thought the storm couldn't get
any darker,
the sun came out and I wept tears of relief,
golden glitter down my cheeks
sometimes life gets so bitter
we forget that it can be sweet

Appreciate Today

When there are bills to pay
& the living room is beginning to rot
you learn to appreciate today,
& be grateful for what you've got
for you never know
when it may all be lost

My Hometown

The tides of change
have swept up this town,
refused to put it down,
making it clear
once and for all
the past is over now
but the future
is yet to be found

The Best Kind of People

The best kind of people
are the ones who tell you
when there is something
on your face,
tell you why they were late,
ask you if you're okay
& somehow know when
you're not,
listen to you talk,
who hug you even when
you're in a fight
& probably nobody's right,
who don't let fleeting things
get in the way of you & them
because that's what love
really is, my friend

This World Isn't Always Gentle But It Tries

I like when others take the
street-side of the sidewalk,
when laughter is louder
than the ticking of a million clocks,
spending Winter days
inside in the warmth in
sweaters and socks
Gray days when the rain
finally stops
and a beautiful and lively
sunset stretches across the skies
just like the laughter creased
corners around our eyes,
reminding us that though
this world is not always gentle,
it tries

We Do the Impossible Like It Is Hopscotch

Life is the rarest thing in the universe
Every single second in the history of the world
has led up to this moment in which we breathe,
our hearts beat
we wake up every morning and every night we fall
asleep
We often forget just how precious and poetic this life
we live is
but we come from the dust of a far away star,
we invented light switches just to mirror it
The chances of life are so small,
there may not be another planet in the entire universe
which can support it,
and yet here we are
on planet earth, our home
So do what makes you wake everyday with a smile
on your face,
chase your dreams, be free
Anything is possible, we have already defied the
odds by existing
We do the impossible like it is hopscotch on a
Summer afternoon
just by living
So take chances
for if you don't, your wishes will never be granted
If you stretch your wings you may fall, but if you
don't you will never fly
of course, it takes courage to reach the sky
but does it not take courage to accomplish anything
in this life?

Everything in the history of the universe went right
from our ancestors, to the birth of the stars that shine
in the night
in order for us to live, and be given these chances
which we decide
to take or to push aside
This life is precious, though often we may find
ourselves forgetting
we have already defied the odds by living
we do the impossible just by existing

Reese Lieberman

The Present Is Speaking Louder

I used to dream of becoming an astronaut
& who knows?
Maybe I will someday
but I guess I've realized that there
are a whole lot of things to explore here
on earth first,
in fact there are so many firsts
I am yet to encounter
I haven't forgotten about the past
but now the present is speaking louder
It's like I've been searching for
who I'd like to be & finally I have
found her
I'm not saying that I'm perfect,
I'm far from it
but it's like there is a light in the distance
& I am running towards it,
getting closer with every step
so I just keep running more & more
now that I have met her
I know I am not there yet, but I am
capable of becoming her
& that just might be even better

Accept the Waves as They Come

Listen to the waves as they
crash and rise
Watch as the sun moves across
the turquoise skies
Smell the sea salt
in the air
Feel the breeze dance lightly
across your cheeks and
through your hair
Taste this precious moment,
walk across the beaches
leaving footprints in the sand
Reach into the ocean,
feel the waters on your hand
Let your hair blow in the wind
Let the sun shine on your skin
Dance, you needn't be a ballerina
just move and sway like the palm trees
and the verbena
Sing like the birds in the blue sky
Let this moment become one
with you,
like the blood in your heart
that courses through your veins
to the tip of your toe –
accept the waves as they come
and respect them when
                              they go

The Beauty of Today

How theatrical is the day
in which I have the ability to say
a thousand words,
watch the palm trees sway,
listen to the elegant songs
of the birds

How beautiful is the silence
that allows music to play

Unbound by Yesterday

Let us wake with the sunrise,
watch the sunset with wonder,
gaze at the stars
and sleep under the moon

Let us not forget who we are
and we can never be lost
Let us walk
into the new day without the taint
of the day before,
just as the sun rose this morning
unbound by yesterday
This moment is a lovely place
to stay

What We Could Be

Allow yourself to change,
for change is the only way
to grow
Sometimes we must let go
of pieces of who we once were
in order to become who
we could be
Though it may not be easy
and breezy
growth can only happen
when you allow change to
occur and therefore are free
You see, just watch as
trees let go of their leaves,
stretch their branches
like a bird's wing
allowing Winter to turn into
Spring

Just the Same

Our footprints may not look
the same,
mine are bare and plain
yours have grooves
from shoes tightened and laced
but just like that
when the tide came,
they were erased
never to be retraced,
we won't ever walk in their
place again
just the same

Our fires may burn different
shades of red,
but when it is done
ashes are all that is left
of every flame

We've Got Today

Infinity is out of reach
but we've got today
and that's enough for me
Let's go for a walk
on the beach,
we'll spot jellies
and splash each other,
notice the hunger
in our bellies
and get ice cream —
it's Summer after all
Let's watch the leaves
change color
when it fades to Fall,
we'll wear cardigans
in Winter
and drink hot cocoa,
coffee, or tea
and when Spring comes
back flourishing
we'll pick flowers,
press their petals
or keep them in a jar —
let's savor our little
slice of forever
wherever we are

This Moment Is Sweeter Than Memories

Memories are sweet
but this moment now is sweeter
in which our hearts beat
and we get to decide
who it is that we want to be
Regret lives in retrospect,
in the dusty corners of a memory
but today holds promise
and possibility

It is crisp like an Autumn breeze
Happiness comes in the smiles,
the laughs, the wordless conversations
our eyes have
Memories are brilliant things,
but they are bittersweet
because in them time stands still
and we freeze,
while in this moment now
we are free
to live, to laugh, to love,
and to be happy —
this moment is so much sweeter
than memories

Reach For the Stars

How could you possibly reach
for the stars
without reaching out your arm
into the dark?
Uncertainty is scary
but so is being sedentary

The End is Just the Beginning

The end of the universe looks
a lot like the start,
things bend & break
until eventually they fall apart
Stars that come from dust
become dust once more
in a big explosion of energy &
light
but from the ruin the rubble
will form new stars,
new life-sustaining forces
in the dark, dark universe
& as it turns out the end
is actually the reverse

Space, Time, and Stars

Stop and look at the stars
remember where you are
All the planets near and far,
so many questions yet to
be answered
and even more yet to be asked
The moments fly by fast
do not let them pass
you by
Breathe, the same air
that started in the sky
in the trees
in the algae
in the seas
Do not be afraid to just be,
be in the moment
be yourself
be happy, be glad
be disappointed, be sad
be a million other things
for that is what it is
to be human
on this great blue planet
in the universe of
time, space, and stars
and your mind, soul, and arms
Do not forget, sometimes
great things happen in the dark

Walk a Little Slower

Fresh air
and blue skies
Turquoise waters
and butterflies
it is on days like this
that you walk a little slower,
look around more
focus less on where
you are going
and pay attention
to where you are

Live For Today

Focus less on tomorrow
and more on today
Say what you need to say
Feel the breeze on your face
This isn't a race,
go at your own pace
and you will find
a single grain
of sand has more to offer
than you think
and do not worry
if the skies are gray,
dancing is an old friend of rain

Big Hearts and Big Dreams

Never underestimate the importance
of little things
after all, in the grand scheme of things
we're all just little things
on a little planet
in a big universe, most of which
remains unseen
with big hearts and big dreams,
eyes wide as can be
and that's enough for you and me

Connected

Feet planted firmly
on the surface of the Earth
Eyes the very color of the dirt
that nurtures the seed
that eventually becomes
the tree
that releases the oxygen
we breathe
you and me
are more connected than
we seem

What Makes Us Different?

Are the songbirds in the sky
not a lot like you and I?

Do they not fight to fly
just as we fight to the end of time
not just to survive
but to thrive?

Are you and I
not a lot like black bears
who too have mountains to climb
and things to do before they sleep?
Are the cliffs they climb
not just as steep
as the ones traversed by you and I?

Are we not all like bees
in a hive,
doing our duties in order to survive
and to be strong?
But also forever longing to belong,
what makes us different from
birds of song?

Love Only Grows

The beautiful thing about love
is that once you love someone
I don't think you ever stop
Even if it's an old friend
you haven't talked to in years
or months
for love is not dictated by a
clock nor a map
that's why distance has no impact
For the human heart has
a language of its own,
and an ever-expanding dictionary,
and your chest is its home
You were born with seeds
in your heart
with the capability to blossom
into a rose
or perhaps an entire forest,
and therefore love only grows

her soul is a river

the weight of the world could not weigh her down
  the blood of her ancestors courses through her veins
    she has been silenced and shunned but that's over now
      she has kept quiet for years, never again will she hide,
        as she did for so long, keeping her voice inside
          her soul is a river, long and wide
        she's tearing down the levee
        that blocks the current of her tide
       for years she has waited to be saved
      by someone else
  now as she lets go of the waves
she realizes that the person she always
needed was herself
and now the weight of the world
could not weigh her down
for she has carried the weight of their words
 and the ones she kept inside
   she is no longer invisible, and she will no longer hide
   because for the first time in her life
     she sees herself, for all her strength and her scars
      she will no longer cower in the background
        as though she is merely a satellite orbiting Mars
         for she knows that she shines with the light
          of all the stars

Linger In This Moment

Do not forget to breathe
and dance
and sing
and linger joyfully
in this moment
before its passing

Look a little longer,
slow down more frequently,
laugh, cry
and please never leave
without saying goodbye

Resilient

Sometimes life pushes us down
but progress is not linear
nor is the path that led me here

and I know there will be many
more bumps in the road,
mornings when the sun doesn't
emerge from behind the clouds,
sleepless nights
where rest feels like water in
a desert,
and days when nothing seems
to be going right

I also know that
every time I have fallen,
I have picked myself back up,
wiped off the dirt,
and decided to start over again
and I trust myself do the same
in the future

There is no predicting the
challenges that may come my
way
but I think it's safe to say
I wouldn't want to be anybody
else at the end of the day

and after all, they say every
broken bone heals stronger
than ever before,
so as I look back at everything
that I have been through
I do not focus on the fleeting
thoughts that these things
could happen again,
and I could be less lucky
next time

but rather the fact that I
made it through it all
because I am capable
and held my head high

I used to be resilient
and once again today I choose
to be resilient

I hope you can see your
own strength and enduring
spirit
you have been through a lot
and healing takes time
maybe you're still in the
process,

but I want you to know this:
what doesn't kill you
just might make you stronger
but being strong
doesn't mean being any less soft

it's easy to be angry at
the world,
especially in challenging
times
but that won't make it hurt
any less
nor will it make the world
any more kind

and the world could certainly
use more kindness
but you know what?
you can be it
you can hold the door
for strangers,
watch sunrises,
listen to birdsong,
because despite all
of the sharp edges there
are still the gentle parts
of this world,
just watch and you will
see them soothe the anger

I know that life can be
scary,
a lot of things are out
of our hands
but what you can control
is what you fill them with,
will it be love
or will you clench them
into fists?

will you look for light
on the dark nights
and find that you can
see the stars
or complain that it's
too dark?

Life will still be scary,
no matter what you decide
like a roller coaster ride
except it is real life
and there is no exit sign,
no way to stop the motion
of this fast moving car

but **I hope you know
just how brilliantly
resilient you are**

Love Looks Like

Sometimes love
looks a lot like being understood
by one another,
wanting nothing but good
for each other

Sometimes love
looks like taking the left side
of the sidewalk,
closest to the road
Sometimes love
feels like the safety
of home,
the warmth of a blanket
after falling asleep on
the couch

or a reminder to lift up
your head when you slouch
so that you don't miss
all the marvelous things above,
like gorgeous sunsets
and magnificent rainbows

Sometimes love
doesn't look like
a ring or a rose

but "did you drink enough water
today?"
"I believe in you"
"It will be okay"

Sometimes love
looks like making mistakes,
and finding forgiveness
in our overflowing hearts

Sometimes it is encouraging
each other to be better
because "together we'll go far"
Always, it is accepting each other
for who we are

brown eyes

some people think them common, plain,
and mundane
but what I see
is sunlight shining on honey
dripping down the trunk and branches
of a long-standing tree
the ground after pouring rain
soil that nurtures flowers and grass
and sequoia trees and wheat grain
and wooden fences
still standing after a hurricane

some people think them common, plain,
and mundane
I think they resemble the wood that fuels
the flame
the foundations of forests and fields
of flowers
and shelter from rain showers
when it is pouring
the ground that holds the weight of skyscrapers
and towers
some people think they're boring,
I think they resemble light in the darkest of hours

Unfinished Work of Art

You are like an unfinished work of art
Still learning to love with your beating heart
Still learning to get back up after you
fall apart
Still anticipating all the adventures
you are yet to experience
Still magnificent and mysterious
You are like a scrapbook,
Picking up new pieces every day
From the letters you send
And the people to whom you wave
Every teardrop is a new splash of paint
Every smile is a star shining in the dark
Illuminating all the love in your heart
You are an unfinished work of art

Synonymous With Love

When all is said and done,
it's nice to be human
to watch the setting sun
and then rise with it in the morning
and watch it all happen again
It's nice to be human
to celebrate birthdays
and meet strangers who in time
might become our very best friends
It's nice to be human
to sit here with pen in hand,
to walk, to run, to stand,
to laugh and to cry
all while existing under the very
same sky
as every single person that's come
before you and I
It's nice to be human
it's nice to write, to ride my bike,
to learn new songs on my guitar,
to research what exactly it is
that makes rockets fly —
it's nice to try
It's nice to tell the people you love
that you love them
to dance
and take those would've-been
missed chances

Humans have always been synonymous
with love
and it's nice when we remember
to utilize this wonderful gift that
we've been granted

Stay Soft

Let your hair down
take your shoes off
Your eyes sparkle
your heart is soft
and so is this world,
despite its bruises
and calluses

it's not broken,
it's just balancing

The Tapestry of My Life

Fresh air makes everything better
There are moments when I think
a hug just might be able to
fix anything,
of course it can't
but for a moment it does
Our lives are really just
a tapestry of moments,
I want mine to be interwoven
with love,
threaded with trust
I'm not completely sure
who holds the needle,
maybe it's the universe
or perhaps it is us,
regardless I've got the people
I love
and that is enough

The Best Version of Me

I want to be the best version of me
the one who wakes early,
for the sunrise is her favorite sight to see
The one who annotates books with
a glittery gel pen
She's a reliable friend,
and a sister on whom you can depend
She strives to make the best of everything
and when she falls apart
she puts herself back together quickly
She's far from perfect,
but she tries her best nonetheless
and that's what makes her different
from the rest
of the people she could've been
She talks a lot when she's happy
She could probably write a hundred million
poems about the sea,
she is free
and the best part of all,
I think she just might be me

Serendipitously Sweet

I sit here gazing upon the skyline
there's a breeze
and an endless amount of trees
emerging from the horizon
I witness the crescendo of many
lifetimes of palms,
the wind in their fronds
a world flourishing with green
and blue
and twice a day
orange, violet, and pink too
and don't forget gold,
gentle yet bold
like the footprints left behind by
your feet
some endings are bitter,
but then again they have to be
before they can become surprisingly,
serendipitously, sweet

Open Heart

Do not grow scales
around your heart,
you are not a
sculpture made of stone
but a living, breathing
work of art
and this little blue planet
we call home
is your canvas

Stages

the sound of the ocean
and the scent of sea salt
freedom
and worries coming to a halt
this is what it's like
to be alive
where chaos meets calm
i'm not flawless and i don't
consider that a fault
for neither is this world
and yet it is simultaneously a sight to behold,
several billion stories to
be told,
and a whole lot more yet to
unfold
it's far too large to hold,
except in pieces,
sand, water, flower petals,
leaves, hands
and felt in warmth, in rain,
in breezes
this is the ink that will someday
stain
the pages
we are all just butterflies
going through stages,
metamorphosis
and i cannot imagine anything
more beautiful than this

Laughter

The memories will echo
forever after
for the times we treasure
are the times of laughter
Smile lines are divine,
for they are reminders
of the moments in time
that are felt rather than
defined

There Is A Place For Writing

It is within everything
It is in the living room while my family talks
about movies they have and
haven't watched
It is outside while the neighbors mow their lawn
(for what seems like the 5th time this week)
It is at the beach
It is in my bedroom with classical music
playing
It is in public places
with lots of unfamiliar faces
It is right here, right now
in the car with the windows down,
as the radio plays in the background
There is a place for writing
and it is waiting to be found,
or rather discovered, between you and the paper
It is not a matter of where or when
pick up the pencil or the pen
There is a place for writing and it starts within

Poetry is a Light

poetry is second nature to me, like my first name
it has a place inside of me, it has made a home
within my veins
without it, i'd be like traffic without street signs,
stoplights, or yellow and white lines
not knowing when to drive and when to patiently sit
poetry is a candle that at any moment may be lit
if darkness befalls me, poetry is a light and i search
for it
like a sailor searches for a lighthouse
poetry is a puzzle, and i am the one who makes
every last piece fit
poetry has made a home inside me, and maybe, just
maybe, a small part of me has found a home inside
of it

Our Souls Are Full

There will be no famine
in our souls
we've got cells of red and white
coursing through our veins,
enlivening our blood
We open our eyes wide
and even when they're shut
we reminisce on this world
with no lack of love
in our hearts
and no deficit of livelihood
in our souls
that muscle in our chests
keeps fluttering
that oxygen keeps a steady
flow, no stuttering
in and out, in and out
Our words echo through the halls,
our laughter reverberates,
we are warmed by the touch
of our intertwined fates,
the moments just as sweet
as amber-colored honey—
our souls will not be going
hungry

Beautiful Things

I love the way we share glances when
looking at things of great beauty
as though to ask silently
"are you seeing what I see?"
Do you ever stop and think to yourself
when looking at a sunset or a sunrise
or looking up at mountainsides
"beautiful things are so much more beautiful
with someone by my side than they
could ever be
if you weren't here with me"

Happiness is…

the smile I don't even notice
on my face,
being together regardless
of the circumstance & place,
it is effortless like a breeze
blowing through my hair
it feels like a breath of fresh air
It is warm & bright,
it looks like daylight
it tastes sweet
it smells like lavender or the
sea
or the living room or latkes
because happiness will follow,
if invited, wherever you
may be
for happiness is making the
best of everything,
no matter what
even on rainy days bluebirds
sing,
brightening the world &
perhaps even showing it a
little bit of love

Dreams are…

the footprints we leave
in the sand,
washed away quickly,
like ice melting on the
palm of your hand
one moment solid,
the next moment droplets
& then gone
unless we choose
to be like the oak tree
in a front lawn.
roots growing deep
& strong
immovable if we choose
to hold on
for when we decide
to plant the seeds
of our dreams,
to nurture them until
they're lush
they can't be lost
because they become
a vital part of us

There Is Light

There may be no promises in this life
but there is light
        & love
        & science
        & seasons
        & the sun
        & hugs
        & handwritten letters
        & stars
        & billions of chances
        that things will get better
        & family
        & friends
        & the knowledge that after the sun
        sets it will rise again
        & millions of other wonderful things
so no, there may not be promises in this dark
universe that is the creator of life
but surely there is light

Never Stop Looking

The sound of seagulls and
crashing waves
The breeze blows gently
on my face
Everything looks golden
in the sun's rays,
even my windblown hair
It's only August but there
is almost a hint of Autumn
in the air
Fresh air feels nice
and the sunset is so very
beautiful,
a reminder of just how
precious and magnificent
this life is
I don't want to spend
another second being
indecisive
I just want to explore,
and to love,
and to never stop looking
around, below, and above

Let It Be

Let the past be the past
Let the present be the present
For who knows what
the future might hold,
there are so many stories
yet to unfold
for they must be written
before they can be told

Early Morning

The feeling of fresh air,
the sound of bird calls,
the white moon still out
in the early morning
Blue skies,
everything feels right
and alive
and excited to be so
I can feel the trees grow,
ever so gently the breeze blows,
the ground beneath my toes
is alive
and seems to be inviting
the whole world to thrive

Together

humans, like art, are not meant
to be compared
our love was made to be shared
our hands fit perfectly in each
other's hands,
we create language after language
all to better understand
one another
and even then, it is not enough
that's why we have music, that
can communicate things words
never could
and art
and our hearts are so very full
of love
and our bodies are all composed
of flesh and blood
from the dust of the very same
stars,
so alike yet we convince ourselves
that we are different
we're not so different after all
we all fall,
and we all bleed the color red
we should strive to help each
other to become better,
and then we, as a family,
as a people, as a society,
as a human race,
will become better

we are all brushstrokes, beautiful
and unique on our own,
but brilliant and bedazzling
together

Letting Go

Sometimes letting go
means letting the tears flow,
letting out what you've been
keeping inside for so long
Sometimes letting go
means realizing
that you've been holding on

We Can Learn

everything looks different in sunlight
the trees, the never-ending streets,
even eyes,
everything seems more alive

there are still shadows,
but darkness and light are old friends,
like stories chase after beginnings
and ends
like a photographer and their trusty lens
like a window and a valance,
letting in just enough light and
not keeping in too much dark
it's a simple thing when you
really think about it — balance
just like shadows and forests
and the sun's ray,
but nobody was born a tightrope walker,
were they?

Remembrance

I am so alive
with the people & the places
I have loved
Who would I be
if it weren't for
my little brown desk?
I know it sounds silly,
but that was the place
where I truly learned
to write
When I think back to those
sticky note filled afternoons
it all comes back to me,
fast & bright,
like a meteorite
because those days
shaped me,
changed me,
that spark of inspiration
once started has become
a roaring flame
I will never be the same
& it's in times of
remembrance such as this
that I am grateful humans
are ever so capable
of change

Real Things Take Time

The bird does not simply soar
into the sky
without first learning to fly
The caterpillar must transform
into the butterfly over time
The sequoia tree starts out as a
sapling not an inch high
The salmon must learn to swim
against the tide
The moon lives in phases,
and as for flowers that bloom
at night
perhaps they gave up hope that
pollinators will come
in daylight
like a knight in shining armor,
though that would be quite a sight
it is also a fairytale,
real things take time
and patience
growth takes waiting
and learning takes the realization
that you do not know it all,
this admittance is a strength
not a fault
for if the bird leapt into the sky
thinking it could fly
without even trying
certainly it would fall

Reese Lieberman

Those who climb Mount Everest
are not simply skilled at the climb,
sequoia trees are not purely strong,
a caterpillar is not born a butterfly
real things, such as you and I
take time

Remember You Are Human

In the midst of a hurricane,
on the brink of ruin
remember you are human
and it is the weather,
things change and they get better

On stormy seas
in a midnight breeze
remember more often than not
we get what we need
not because things simply
work out
but because we are human,
we make flowers bloom in
deserts,
we figure out where others' wounds
hurt
and make them better

We are human,
flesh and bone, imperfect and all
Decorated with flaws
but wise enough to look at
this world in awe
We are not gods,
but we are innately talented
at beating the odds

There is a Way

Often when it feels like there is
no way out
there is a way
beyond what you ever imagined
not impossible nor invisible
but easy to overlook or ignore
that you'd never seen before —
it's difficult to find a road
if you are always searching for
a door

What You've Become

I hope you are proud
of every dark and scary,
seemingly endless night
you made it through
Every day when it felt like
the skies wouldn't turn blue,
instead they opened up
and poured on you
but you know what?
You opened your eyes
in the morning and
made it through
with or without the sun
and most importantly,
I hope you're proud
of what you've become

Scars Are Evidence

Are our scars not evidence
that we did so much more
than exist?
That we fell and got hurt
then got back to our feet
and wiped off the dirt
Perhaps a hand reached out to us,
and perhaps when others
were down
we reached out to help them
and were never the ones
to push them to the ground,
but help them to their feet
and now we give people
bandages when they bleed
and hold doors for strangers,
never knowing where they might lead
and maybe when you look
down at your untied shoelaces,
you'll remember the scraped knee
you got when you were young
and naive
Perhaps every scar
is evidence meant to remind us
of how we got this far

Water & Dirt

Shadows play games
with the sunshine
Gold flowers bloom
Birdsong drifts lazily
across the breeze
thick like honey
through the hives
of striped bees
Leaves fall gently
down to earth
so much life starts out
as water & dirt

An Embodiment of the Earth

This giant beneath my back
is steady
indelible but a giver of so
much life
Roots so indiscernibly deep
yet a few peaks rise above
the dirt
a birthplace,
a shelter,
a sanctuary,
for crimson tipped birds,
the delicate dahlias,
a playground for the brown-tailed
squirrels
It provides & it receives,
an embodiment of the Earth
just as waves rise & recede
constantly giving & taking
from this amaranthine universe —
carbon dioxide in exchange for oxygen,
taking up space while simultaneously
supplying it
for the fair-colored foxes,
the majestic hawks when they
need a break from flying &
the ants who just might be more evolved
than us
& the moss
& the unruly caterpillars
who will soon metamorphosize
into elegant butterflies

Unmistakably Human

It takes up a miniscule chunk of the Earth,
ginormous or microscopic
by needless comparison
but it opens its branches far & wide,
cultivating so very much life
with every fallen leaf, every moment
it stands unshakably high
improving this evergreen world
around it & inside

Surrounded by Her Symphony

Light shining through trees
Breathing in the mountain breeze
The rushing water is almost all I hear
as Mother Earth falls to her knees
bending and shaping the world
however she may please
I am surrounded by the color green,
the scent of flowing water,
and pine needles
I hold onto the railing and find
several beetles
crawling along the edge, I don't identify
the type
Again, the trees are graced by the delicate
touch of sunlight
Still, Mother Earth falls and flows,
following gravity's law
or perhaps inventing it
and once more I watch in awe

It Is Beautiful (written at Lake Erie)

The rocky coast
beneath my toes
there is shelter on a stone
for a dragonfly and ladybug both
hiding or resting from the wind
that blows my pulled-back hair
and touches my skin
It is fresh and alive
there is energy that comes with the tide
I've forgotten about traffic
and stop signs
there is freedom here
in the breeze, in the sunshine,
in the waters as they come and go
like a magnet being pushed and pulled
like the pages of a book as they unfold
All I hear is the waves
and the wind fighting against my ears
the skies are clear
it is peaceful here but not lazy
it is blues it is grays it is yellows it is gold it is
specks of silver in the stones
it is birds taking flight
it is the ladybug that just landed on my shorts
and now is crawling on my fingers as I write
it is beautiful and it is life

Language of the Trees

I long to learn the language
      of the trees
to speak softly & with ease
to tread lightly
      through the breeze
to live deeply
& bear fruits
to welcome change
with open limbs
all while holding steadfastly
to my roots

When Living Becomes Loving

I love love
I love the way people's faces
light up
when they talk with passion
even if I don't understand,
I can always listen and imagine
I love treating others with
compassion
the more you love, the more you
live —
I mean truly take it in
You are more likely to notice
the freshly flourishing blossoms
and buds
if you tend to them with a watering
can or misty spray
you'll start to see gray skies
as so much more than rain
And that spark within your eyes
is surely not to fade
in fact it grows brighter
every single day

Nourishment

The more you nourish the world
around you
the more it nourishes
you too

Chasing Tomorrow

Isn't tomorrow such an inviting
word
like an open door?
Glistening with possibility,
with just as much allure as
yesterday
but without the confines of history
only memories yet to be made
and decisions yet to be tainted
by yes or no
x or y
Isn't it wonderful to think that
yesterday's stranger
could be tomorrow's friend?
What once was a dead end
could be an open road,
just think of the adventures
upon which you are yet to go
Tomorrow really is a magical place,
it really is a shame
that we could spend our whole lives
chasing tomorrow, that empty space
and never get anywhere at all
when all the while today,
with all of tomorrow's wondrous
qualities stares us in the face

Look A Little Closer

Isn't it a funny world
we live in?
We're so similar yet we
fail to see it, too busy
pointing out our differences
well I won't spend my life
letting these silly little things
get in the way,
will you?
At the end of the day,
we are all human
and that is one thing I will
always know to be true
There really isn't more to it
because quite honestly
I love our differences
I love when others have
different music taste than me
because often I find myself
falling in love with songs
I would've never listened to
and when I look at you
I'm not looking for pieces
of myself,
there are mirrors for that
I love that your handwriting
curves at different points
than mine
We wake up at different times
and perhaps different places

but our home will always be
this one earth
and our shadows, undeniably similar,
are created by the very same sun
We read different genres of books
but really we're doing the same thing
paper and ink
become the stories
into which we sink
Look a little closer and you will see
even our differences are a lot more alike
        than you think

Reese Lieberman

Infinity in a Hug

Did you know that infinity
can sometimes be found in a hug?
For it shouts,
ever so sweetly,
like someone calling out your name
gentle, like the wings of a dove
& it comes like a flood

> *you are loved,*
> *you are loved,*
> *you are loved*

A Very Welcome Guest

Love is warm
it comes unexpectedly
like the moon
in the daytime
like calm seas
at high tide
like a very welcome guest,
the knock that comes as a surprise
on your front door,
headlights illuminating your porch
Love is flowers that bloom
in surreal places
like sidewalk cracks & moldy basements
in alleyways, finding sanctuary
& creating stability in a state
of displacement
Love does not always come
with grandeur,
it is elegant, of course
not necessarily like a vineyard
but a single, simplistic & idealistic
rose
after all, every forest
starts with one little seed
& it sure is lovely
to watch as it grows

True Love

True love transcends time and space
The distance makes no difference
because love is not a place
It is harmony between two beings

Time and space are like the seasons,
they come and go
but love continues through sleet and snow,
through the highs and lows,
true love is like a river that endlessly flows,
or a star that eternally glows

It is bigger than any time
or place on planet earth
true love is the strongest force
in the universe

The Beauty of Change

I have found happiness,
I have found the sun
& on days like this
I feel as if my life
has only just begun
I'm a new flower in a
fresh field
orchids grow, violets
blossom
leaves once curled
& tones of copper
have transformed into
a brilliant shade of green
birds fly as though
on a fresh pair of wings
Change really can be
a beautiful thing

Life's True Meaning

Things change quickly,
but sometimes these changes
are for the better
life is like the weather

Sometimes the sun sets
revealing a whole world
of colors
hidden by the day
Sometimes we find ourselves
astray
but in the end,
we always find our way
in the end,
it will be okay

Sometimes we must wander
that does not make us lost
At times we ponder
and the world feels as small
as the one inside our thoughts,
but it is not

Sometimes it feels like the ground
is slipping from beneath
our feet
like the earth's plates
are shifting
and leaving us behind

Unmistakably Human

Whenever you feel this way
remember in your chest
your heart continues to beat
focus on the precious air in your lungs
as you breathe

Sometimes you have to
step away from the driver's seat
and simply walk on the earth
beneath your feet

Changes come and go
like the seasons
Sometimes we get lost searching
for the reasons
but life's true meaning
is to evolve and to love
Sometimes we lose our way
but a mother always finds
her way back to her son,
just watch the ways of the dove

When you get lost look around
and above
at this world which we are all
a part of

Changes come and go
with or without reasons
but when you look up at the stars
you will find life's true meaning

Reese Lieberman

We are meant to find light
inside the dark
after all, we are children of the cosmos,
us little human beings
just like the lilies, the lilacs,
and the leaves of the biggest oak trees
we are meant to change
with the seasons
We are meant to let our hair blow
in the breeze

Flight is for the dove,
the true meaning of our lives
is to **evol**ve and to love

Encircled by Life

Everything in motion,
waves form in the
winding runoff from the ocean
I am encircled by sunlight
and water
at the brink of so much life,
insects chirping,
birdsong cascading
from the trees,
dolphins splashing
so very alive and free
Fish jump,
pelicans hunt,
butterflies flutter through the
light breeze
I am surrounded by so very
much life
and there is so very much life
within me

Infinite

You never know what
tomorrow might bring
but what you do know
is that even on the
gray mornings
bluebirds sing,
on the long days the sun
sets,
a wonderful display
of color
your eyelids find their way
back to each other
over & over again
There is so much light
in this world, my friend
so much life to be lived
& most importantly
so much love to be given
All we've really got is
the present
we're lucky enough to have
been gifted
& it sure feels like a lot
when your heart beats
for something
like it does
when you open it to love
Nobody knows what tomorrow
might bring

it could be different
than we can even imagine,
it could be made of
soon to be regrets
or composed of memories
we won't want to forget
but as long as we've got
each other
this moment feels pretty
infinite,
doesn't it?

Can't You See?

Darling,
you may not have seen it
but ever since the start
you have been a work
of art
the more you welcome love
into your heart
the more layers of oil
you add to your masterpiece,
you see
you don't have to be finished
in order to be complete

you can breathe

the waters look treacherously
            deep
    until you dive in
  & realize
        that if you stick your head up
  to the surface
you can breathe

life isn't always as daunting
            as it seems

she danced to music

she was caught between
wanting to feel every ounce of time,
every droplet of water in the ocean
against her skin,
a longing to take it all in —
and wanting to escape it,
to breathe, to be,
to run, to dance under moonlight, to sit
under the limbs of a tree
she was caught between wanting
everything and nothing,
wanting to feel time and to escape it,
she chose not to run away from it
instead she danced to music,
with dignity and grace,
spending her time with a smile on her face
unafraid that she might lose it,
because that is exactly how you lose it —
by being afraid
instead she danced to music.

There is love in everything we do

Love slips between the cracks
like light
through half opened blinds
into everything we do
it is so much more tangible
than something solely processed
by the mind
because love flows through the
heart
to every part of your body
and therefore is transferred
to everything you touch
love is imperfect but not impractical
it is flawed but nonetheless
true
and beautiful
and it is present in every single
thing we do

A Second Chance

and what if you were to quite simply
breathe in happiness
like the fragrance of flowers?
with no limitations or expectations
that these are the golden days
or the joyful hours?
what if you just let life be what it is
and therefore what it could be
forget about your ideas of
what it should be
perhaps if you let go of your worries
and held tighter to your dreams
you would see the sunshine
and perhaps you have been missing
it all this time,
looking for fireworks instead
and therefore rendering yourself blind
but you see light
comes in many forms,
just as most things in this life
love, for example, doesn't always fit
a standard design
sometimes it doesn't like to be labeled
"yours" or "mine"
but that doesn't mean it isn't ours
sometimes it is looking up at
the stars,
butterflies replaced by a feeling
of safety and hearts not racing
but finally able to relax

sometimes it is reassurance,
not feeling tongue tied but talking
openly,
sometimes it is someone with whom
to dance,
smile and laugh
and occasionally say things
you can't take back,
sometimes it is a second chance
and if love deserves
a second chance,
despite its mistakes and
messiness —
doesn't happiness?

Ready to Feel

the sweetness of smiles
the softness of sunsets
the effervescent glow of moonlight
the energy and subtlety of sunrises,
how they effortlessly hold so much peace
a light breeze
in my hair, in the trees
how the world keeps turning
ever so slowly it doesn't bother us at all
the warmth of a hot cup of tea in late fall
sweaters and good news
books and breaking out of the blues
waking up
with a smile
carpet beneath my toes rather than tile
singing, letting go and realizing if it's meant to be
it will
there is softness in what used to be hard as steel
there is gentleness in this world, just be patient and
ready to feel

It's the Warmth We Remember

Winter isn't as bitter as people make it out to be,
at least those aren't the parts that I remember
it's the warmth of the fireplace that leaves its ashes
scattered across my memory
it's the mittens that fit just right,
not too big and not too tight
it's the cocoa my mom made
I remember the crisp december air
but its bite was quick to fade
I remember all the board games we played,
trivia, sorry, life, clue, and occasionally charades
I remember the hugs
that made everything feel okay
I remember the love
that was not sprinkled but spread throughout the
halls
I remember my overalls
and boots
watching the world from my car seat, trees,
their changing leaves as they held steadfastly to their
roots
I remember being together,
the laughter, the jokes, there was peace rather than
pressure
and I think that I will keep it with me forever
for it is not the bitter weather,
but the warmth that we remember

Just Be Here

The steps may be small
but it is better than taking
no steps forward at all
I might fall
but I will always keep my
head up
toward the vast skies
even when I feel small
for I have found that even
amidst the grandest depths
of dark
there is light
and perhaps like stars
in the night,
there is so much
love in my heart
it is visible
perhaps I will go far
and maybe I won't know
until I am there
Sometimes it is best
to let the wind blow
in my hair,
watch the ocean ebb and flow
just be here
and forget about tomorrow

A Wild Nature

Light became lost in
the smell of earth, lilacs, and wild nature
The land and the sky,
each and every child of nature
Colors changed, seasons came
and went
The dandelions, the daisies, the songbirds, the
butterflies —
every one of them thrived
and paused for a moment on the day
that Spring arrived
in awe of the way he loved to be alive

Homesick

You say that you're homesick,
tired of traveling,
bored of roads
But darling, how can you be homesick
when *you* are home?

Doorway to Life

Breath is the doorway to life
just as the sunset is to the night
It is the bridge between
living things,
the balance between
the sky and an eagle's wings,
land and sea,
Earth and tree,
breath is the doorway between
you and me

Imperfect and Flawed

I am imperfect and you, my friend, are flawed
I say that without regret
because that's what led us here

Every teardrop,
each moment spent in fear
when the world seemed to stop
Every night spent awake,
and every hour asleep in the realm
of a nightmare —

that is what led us here
to the wind blowing in our hair,
the Summer sun shining on our skin
and brightening the air

Every loss is not magically made into a win
but when embarking on journeys
you are wiser in the end
than when you begin
so live your life without regrets
and please do not forget
even stormy days end in sunsets

the kind of movie you don't watch alone

don't the stars
look the most beautiful
when they shine together
as one,
a constellation?
the trees do not bear fruit
for themselves
but for the bats and the bunnies,
sunflowers grow not just
towards the sun,
but each other
bees are not selfish in the
creation of honey
don't the stars look the most
beautiful when together
they shine?
perhaps likewise,
this world wasn't meant to be
viewed by
a single pair of eyes
nor a singular mind
life is like the kind of movie
you don't watch alone
after all, it is our presence
that makes a place into
a home

To All the People I Will Someday Love But Haven't Met Yet

Right   now   we   are   busy   living   our
own   beautiful,   messy   lives
like   passengers   inside   different   cars
along   the   same   familiar   yellow   lines
but   someday   they   will   become
i   n   t   e   r   t   w   i   n   e   d
like   yarn,
someday   I   might   even   find   shelter
in   your   arms
but   until   then
I   hope   this   world   is   kind   and   friendly,
I   hope   it   treats   you   gently
Keep   living   and   loving   intensely
I'll   see   you   when   it's   meant   to   be

Everlasting

A drop in the ocean
A breath in the wind
We are small yet we are infinite
Miniscule yet everything
But an instant in a universe
Of tragedies & fleeting magic
& yet we are everlasting

The Octet Rule aka the Fundamental Desire to be Whole

the search for stability
electrons seek it in each other
just like we seek strength and shelter
in one another's arms and souls
sulfates and soulmates
ions and finding someone to rely on
life really is a mysterious thing
crystal lattice, precise patterns,
opposite energies,
diamond rings, dances, and
slim chances
they say life imitates art,
well it seems life mirrors life itself
the tides pulled in and out
in and out
up and down and
up again down
the shore
by the sheer force of the moon
the beating of the heart
pump pump pump pump
the breathing of the lungs
in and out
in and out
drawn by the sheer will
of the human body and the
instinct to live

the nebula and the iris,
the latter which poets have spoken of
for centuries,
the prior which has been around
for millennia
only a hundred centuries ago
the octet rule was discovered
long before that we uncovered,
or perhaps invented
or maybe we just welcomed,
love
which is to say that the fundamental
desire to be whole,
goes far beyond having a hand to hold
into the world that shapes us,
and, perhaps it is even applicable
to the very atoms that make us

The Soft Below Rough Edges

This world is so very rough
around the edges
but it's not all rocky cliffs
and scary ledges,
there are colorful sunsets,
wildflowers, gardens, books,
deep conversations, small talk,
comfortable silence, laughter,
safety —
reasons to drop your defenses
Shelter
is not always little houses
with white picket fences
home is not always four walls
but forearms and heartbeats,
fingers intertwined, a silent understanding,
a quiet "I am here" —
reasons your stress-tightened jaw
unclenches
This world is so very raw
and pure
when you dive deeper,
past the rough edges
into the waters, so harmless,
so reckless
so deep, so just breathe,
just be
and you can never be defenseless
if you learn to love the pieces
of this universe,

and hold onto the things you love
like a lion fights for dear,
mysterious, chaotic, lovely life,
let go of resentments
do this, and you will become
the soft below this world's rough edges

Acknowledgements

Thank you to my Grandfather, Ron Lieberman, who inspires me endlessly. Who encourages me always. He makes me want to always keep asking questions and keep learning. He thinks about things on a level that is deeper than I'd ever think of things. I think discussing my poetry with him makes me a better writer. And it also reminds me of the power of words, and, more specifically, poetry. I'd like to thank my grandfather for all of this, and also just for being such an amazing person. Among many other things he taught me that when light particles enter a black hole they become waves. There is good in people, give them a chance. And to make the best of everything, no matter what. Thank you, grandpa.

Thank you to Sharon Lieberman, who is one of the most caring and considerate people anybody could ever know, whom I get to have the privilege to call my Grandmother. She has an endless amount of empathy. She cares so very deeply about people, a rarity in this day and age — one I hope to never take for granted. It is something that cannot be taught or learned, it is who she is. I can only aspire to care as deeply as she does. She has such an open heart, and I think she's the reason I do too. I cherish our conversations. She is the best Grandmother anybody could ever ask for. She truly is a light in the lives of everybody who knows her. Thank you, grandma.

Thank you to my Father, who taught me the true meaning of strength and dedication. I have watched him set his mind to something and never quit. Despite everything, he pushes through every single day, he works to become stronger. He taught me that strength is not something which you possess, but rather a choice you make in every moment. My will and determination come from him. He taught me to always try my best. My Father has not only inspired me but constantly encouraged me to write. He is always happy to read my poems, ever since I started writing. Looking back through old notebooks from when I was eleven years old, to put it simply, it's clear to see the progress I have made since then. But still, my Father has believed in me since I first started writing my silly little poems with misspelled words. And lastly, he is the reason this book is in your hands right now. Thank you, dad.

Thank you to my Mother, who always finds ways to push me. She is the reason why I wrote my first poem when I was eleven years old. I remember she came to me and said, "there

is a poetry contest, I think you should enter."
I said I'd give it a shot and started writing. At
first it was challenging, but I liked that it wasn't
easy. I showed my poems to her. I asked her if
she thought I had any chance of winning; her
encouragement is the reason I submitted them. I
got third place. The prize was that the poems got
posted on a website and I got sent a trophy in
the mail. I still have that trophy, and I remember
how proud it made me feel. But I think the true
prize was poetry. It was finding something that
I love. My Mother has continued to push me,
just like she did that day years ago. She always
encourages me to share my poetry, and I have
never regretted it. Thank you, mom.

Thank you to my sisters, Kyra and
Taylor, who are always there for me no matter
what. They not only played an integral role in
helping me with this book, but also in my life.
Both of them dedicated so much of their time to
helping me with this book, and I am eternally
grateful for that. They are also two of the most
talented writers and artists I know. There are not
better people to laugh with, cry with, or watch
When Harry Met Sally in the eye of a hurricane
with. They are both wonderful human beings,
and I am lucky to be their sister. Thank you,
besties.

I am beyond lucky to have these people
in my life. Without these people I wouldn't be

who I am today and this book certainly wouldn't be what it is, were it to exist at all. I'd also like to thank all of them for taking the time to read my poems. I love all of the people listed above endlessly. Thank you for being your wonderful selves.

Thank you to the Instagram writing community. I have met so many talented writers, and kind people on there, as well as made some great friends. A special thank you to Evan, Purva, Mari, Ingrid (aka Betty), Aaditi, Rory, Jiya, Dhanya, and Drei. You all inspire me.

And lastly, thank you dear reader. I hope that you are every bit as beautiful in your eyes as you are in mine. It's nice to be human, don't you think?

About the Author

Reese Lieberman is a reader, daydreamer, and poet. This is her second collection of poetry, she self-published her first book *this world from my 2 eyez* at fifteen years old. She strives to find the beauty in this world, and share it through her poetry.

For more of her writing, check out @reesewith3e.s on Instagram and TikTok.